Highly Advanced Reading Curriculum

READING
EDGE

E-field Academy

3

Reading gives us insight into our life and helps to visualize our future.
It gives us someplace to go when we have to stay where we are. - *Mason Cooley*

We're

Table of Contents READING EDGE SMART 3

Introduction

Every student knows studying English requires a lot of patience. Even worse, some English books are difficult and boring. Fortunately, there is a way you can change your perspective on learning English. Now you can develop your reading skills in an enjoyable way.

The Reading EDGE Smart series will help you to improve your reading skills. You can learn how to read with a purpose.

Each level of this series comes with one text book, one guide book and one audio component. Each book is organized into 5 units consisting of vocabulary and related questions. One of the key features of this series is that it integrates many skills: reading, vocabulary building, listening and writing.

This series also deals with a variety of unique and interesting topics, and the readings are graded to the appropriate length and depth depending on the English proficiency level of the student.

After reading, students will be challenged to guess the meaning of words used in the passage, summarize the passage, and solve various types of questions.

Students can listen to the entire script by MP3 or use the attached CD. Students will broaden their English ability from reading to listening, speaking and writing. This integrated approach will enable students to dramatically improve their English.

We're Reading EDGE Smart Features

	READING EDGE SMART 1~2	READING EDGE SMART 3~4	READING EDGE SMART 5~6
Unit	Topic based	Korean SAT test based	In-depth reading skill based
Reading skill	Speed Reading	Impact Reading	Power Reading
	Essential skills for reading	Essential skills for preparing for the Korean SAT test	Essential skills for In-depth reading

■ Reading Passages

The Reading EDGE Smart series covers a wide variety of topics ranging from teen life to social issues. This series also covers academic and contemporary topics, which will motivate students to study English. The real life topics will provide students with knowledge and an enjoyable reading experience. In addition, passages related to social issues will give them more insight into everyday life and help foster logical thinking skills. This series has longer passages, consisting of over 300 words, which will help students get used to reading longer passages clearly and confidently.

■ Words

Students are encouraged to read the definitions in English, which provides them greater exposure to English vocabulary. After reading the definitions in English, they are asked to translate them into Korean. This process will motivate students to think in English first, then guess the matching Korean word.

Structure **Vol.3**

■ Question Types

After reading each passage, students are advised to answer questions related to the passage. These questions are meant to help students promote their English comprehension skills. In addition, they are designed for students who are preparing for various types of tests including school tests, college entrance exams and internationally recognized tests such as TOEFL. The question styles used in the Reading EDGE Smart series include multiple choice, fill in the blank and summary completion. The activities in the Reading EDGE Smart will ensure greater reading fluency and exam success. Completing the summary will contribute to improving students' writing skills by enhancing their ability to think in English.

■ Tips

This section provides additional information related to the passages in order to encourage further thought on the topics.

■ Review

This section gives students a chance to practice words and idiomatic expressions learned in each unit using various approaches.

■ Reading Skills Section

The Reading EDGE Smart Series takes three different approaches to developing and improving reading skills: Speed Reading, Impact Reading, and Power Reading. These sections will help students grasp the essential skills required to improve their reading ability.

■ Guide Book

The Reading EDGE Smart Guide Book consists of Korean translations, idiomatic expressions, structure review, grammar tips and answer keys.

Growing up is learning how to deal with difficulties and the benefits are great.

Unit 1

Identifying the Main Idea and the Title

Read the following and answer the questions.

How can we make thousands of people happier by not telling the truth? In 1962, there were only black and white television channels in Sweden. One day, the station's technical expert, Kjell Stensson, appeared on the news to announce that viewers could convert their existing black and white TV sets to display color reception by putting a stocking over them. Stensson lied to thousands of people to perform what is now one of the most famous April Fool's Day hoaxes in Sweden.

There are plenty of theories about the origin of April Fool's Day, although nobody is sure which one is correct. Some people say that April Fool's Day originated in Germany. They say it was first celebrated soon after the adoption of the Gregorian calendar.

In many pre-Christian cultures May Day (May 1) was celebrated as the first day of summer, and signaled the start of the planting season. An April Fool was someone who did this prematurely because they still adhered to the Julian calendar which was replaced in 1582.

Nowadays, April Fool's Day is celebrated with the execution of elaborate practical jokes on (a) _____ (suspect) victims. In most countries, the jokes last only until noon. If you play a trick on someone after this time, then you are the April Fool.

April 1st is an exciting opportunity to think up pranks to play on each other at school or at work. Looking back on the origins of April Fool's Day helps us to understand the history of why we play these hilarious practical jokes.

Words	Read the following definitions and translate them into Korean.

- **convert:** to change (something) into a different form or properties _____
- **reception:** the act of receiving or the state of being received _____
- **hoax:** false, wrong information _____
- **prematurely:** too soon; in a premature manner _____
- **adhere:** to stick to something or keep the idea _____
- **execution:** performance or doing something _____
- **hilarious:** extremely funny _____

Impact reading

1. Which is the best title for the passage?

① What Is April Fool's Day?
② How Can We Make People Happier?
③ How Did Kjell Stensson Lie to People?
④ How Did People Celebrate April Fool's Day?
⑤ What Are the Best Ways to Play Tricks on People?

2. What is the appropriate form of the blank (a)? Use the given word.

_____

3. Write T if the statement is true. Write F if it is false.

① The origin of April Fool's Day hasn't been clarified yet. _____

② Kjell Stensson upset the viewers by lying on a national TV show. _____

③ The Julian calendar was commonly used after the adoption of
   the Gregorian calendar. _____

TIP

Groundhog Day

+ How do you know whether winter has ended or not? In America and Canada,
  Groundhog Day (February 2nd) is a kind of crossroad between winter and spring.
  It is believed that if the groundhog sees its shadow it will be scared and go back
  into its hole. If this happens winter will continue for six more weeks.

Read the following and answer the questions.

When we think about authors, we don't usually put them in the same category as soldiers, bull-fighters or big-game hunters; however, that is exactly what the great writer Ernest Hemingway was. (a) Hemingway led a robust and colorful lifestyle and (b) his writing was greatly influenced by his wartime experiences and his passion for adventure.

In the First World War, he served in the Red Cross Ambulance Corps on the Italian front. He also served in the Second World War, suffering several serious injuries while on the front lines. (c) His war experiences had a lasting effect on his psyche and certainly served as a great inspiration for his writing in novels such as *For Whom the Bell Tolls* and *A Farewell to Arms*.

ⓐ _____ his experiences in war, he led a vibrant lifestyle. His prize-winning novels *The Sun Also Rises* and *Death in the Afternoon* reflect his passion. He was an aficionado of bull-fighting and spent a great deal of time in Spain. He often went on safari and was known as a good shot when hunting for big-game. His experiences in Africa were reflected in the works *Green Hills of Africa* and *The Snows of Kilmanjaro*. His adventurous spirit also resulted in several injuries, most notably his survival of a plane crash while on safari.

(d) Hemingway's life ended with as much drama as his writing embodied. In his later life he suffered from bipolar disease and committed suicide shortly before his 62nd birthday. (e) Still, his name lives on as one of the 20th century's most well-known authors.

| Words | Read the following definitions and translate them into Korean. |

- **robust:** strong, tough, powerful _____
- **psyche:** someone's mind and feelings _____
- **aficionado:** a person who likes something and knows a lot about it _____
- **embody:** to express an idea _____
- **bipolar:** having two strong and opposing opinions or elements _____

Impact reading

1. Which best describes the main idea of the passage? Choose one from (a) to (e)?

_____

2. What is the most appropriate expression for the blank ⓐ?

① Due to
② Similar to
③ Apart from
④ In regards to
⑤ Regardless of

3. Match the main idea with each paragraph.

Paragraph 1 •   • His work was influenced by his wartime experiences.

Paragraph 2 •   • Hemingway was an unusual author.

Paragraph 3 •   • His life ended tragically.

Paragraph 4 •   • His work was influenced by his passion for life.

TIP

Cuba and Hemingway

✦ Even though Hemingway was an American writer, he lived in Cuba for 20 years and wrote some of his masterpieces there, including *The Old Man and the Sea*. What aspects of Cuba attracted Hemingway? Cuba is well-known for rum, cigars and its beautiful scenery. However, its most valuable treasure is its people. Through hard times, they still keep their hope and enjoy what they have in their lives.

Read the following and answer the questions.

The process of making Hanji paper is a long and tedious one, which is hands-on from start to finish. It begins with Mulberry tree bark, which is boiled for hours. Any black bark is removed from the white pulp, which is bleached repeatedly using sunlight and lye. The lye neutralizes the finished paper, allowing it to last for millennia. The final step is to evenly disperse the pulp on a bamboo screen by dipping it into the pulp mixture.

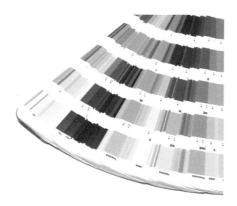

So, what qualities does this precious paper have? (A) When it comes to high quality, Hanji is second to none. (B) Experts agree that in terms of fibers, Korean Mulberry trees have the upper hand over Mulberry trees from China, Japan and the Philippines. (C) One of the most distinctive features of Hanji is its remarkable durability. (D) It can indeed last for over a thousand years, which is why Hanji was used for official government records.

(E) In today's fast-paced world, people have little time or patience to make Hanji using traditional methods. However, once you experience the translucent beauty of a Hanji window, or see some adorable Hanbok made of Hanji, you will understand why artisans are willing to devote their lives to ⓐ _____ .

| Words | Read the following definitions and translate them into Korean. |

- **tedious:** boring and rather frustrating _____
- **hands-on:** requiring manual operation or control _____
- **bleach:** to use a chemical to make something white _____
- **lye:** caustic soda _____
- **disperse:** to spread over a wide area _____
- **durability:** being strong and lasting for a long time _____

Impact reading

1. What is the appropriate title for the article?

① Hanji Making Alarms the World
② Hanji Making and Its Artistic Beauty
③ Paper Making: Preserving Korean Traditions
④ Hanji: A Quality Material for Everyday Items
⑤ Mulberry Trees: The Key Component of Hanji-Making

2. Where does the following sentence best fit?

> Another characteristic is its fine texture and smooth surface, which adds a beautiful sheen to it.

① (A)   ② (B)   ③ (C)   ④ (D)   ⑤ (E)

3. What is the most appropriate expression for the blank ⓐ?

① this expensive work
② this time-consuming process
③ fast-paced lifestyle
④ traditional way of life
⑤ modernizing the process

Paper's Other Uses

+ How do you use paper? Most people think it is just a material to write on or for books. However, paper had many more uses in Korea. In old Korean houses, room doors were made of wood and paper. Not only that, paper also played an important role in the kitchen. Surprisingly, paper was used as a pot lid. It prevented insects and dust from getting into the pot and prevented the food from drying out.

Read the following and answer the questions.

(A) ⓐ _____?
Toys such as balls, puzzles, bowling sets, yoyo's and dolls are a fun way for children to build these important skills. These toys have been around since ancient times, and are still enjoyed by children today! Of course, there have been some changes in production and materials: balls are now made of rubber instead of stone, puzzles out of cardboard instead of ivory, and dolls have almost as many outfits as their owners. Despite these modifications, classic toys continue to provide children with the same benefits as their predecessors: motor skills, co-ordination, sharing and creativity.

(B) ⓑ _____?
Video and computer games have found their way to the top of children's wish lists, and most children would choose a gaming system over a ball or a jump rope. There has been substantial controversy surrounding the effects of gaming on children. Some people argue that these high-tech toys are addictive and bad for mental and physical health. However, it cannot be denied that they are fun. Recently, physically interactive systems such as the Wii and intellectual games like Brain Age are winning over critics. These games increase motor skills while helping children learn.

(C) ⓒ _____?
If you've ever seen children building sandcastles at the beach, you'll know the answer is no. Natural "toys" such as sand, soil, snow and water can keep children entertained for extended periods of time. Activities such as building sandcastles or snowmen can help children learn teamwork as they work towards a common goal. Since the possibilities are endless with these playthings, children are able to enjoy limitless creativity while learning how to co-operate and interact with each other.

Impact reading

1. What is the passage mainly about?

① The history of toys

② How toys can benefit children

③ How children can have more fun

④ How children can develop social skills

⑤ Why children should give up certain toys

2. What are the appropriate sentences for blanks ⓐ, ⓑ and ⓒ?

- Do kids need high-tech toys to have a fun time?
- How can parents keep their children from being addicted to high tech toys?
- How can children learn many of the physical, mental and social skills?
- Are classic toys still a favorite amongst children?
- What are the ways of learning various skills they need other than toys?

ⓐ _____

ⓑ _____

ⓒ _____

| Words | Read the following definitions and find the words in the passage. |

- a person who worked before someone: _____
- ability to move: _____
- large amount of something: _____
- allowing communication between sender and receiver: _____
- happening for a long period of time: _____
- having no boundary and worries of running out: _____

Read the following and answer the questions.

Have you ever star-gazed at night and wondered where you fit in amongst the vast universe? Chances are your answer is 'yes.' If so, you're not alone. In fact, people have been asking this same question for years. One of the most interesting examples of humankind's curiosity about the constellations can be seen in the ancient Egyptian Pyramids of Giza.

Ancient Egyptians had a great interest in astrology. In fact, the constellation which we know as Orion was called Sah by these ancient people. They believed that Sah was the final destination of their dead kings.

One of the most prominent theories about the Egyptian Pyramids was put forth by Robert Bauval, a prominent researcher of the pyramids. He claimed that the pyramids were much more than just tombs for Pharaohs. According to Bauval, these pyramids were designed as part of a master plan to mirror the layout of the constellations. He contended that the positioning of the Pyramids of Giza on the ground was correlated to the position of the stars in the sky.

The placement of the pyramids in relation to the stars was, according to Bauval, a way for the deceased king to travel to the afterworld. Therefore, by aligning the tombs and the stars, they could create a path for the king to travel along. According

to the legend, each dead king was represented by a star in the constellation Sah. Therefore, the pyramids, which served as Earthly tombs for the dead kings, were positioned in a way so as to represent the specific star that each deceased king became in Sah.

The relationship between the Pyramids of Giza and Sah can teach us a lot about the ancient Egyptians. We now understand their reasoning behind the positioning of the pyramids, as well as their relationship with the afterlives of their dead leaders.

Impact reading

1. What is the best title for the passage?

① Ancient Egyptians' Belief in the Afterlife
② The Giza Pyramids and Their Scientific Basics
③ Ancient Egyptians and Their Advanced Architecture
④ Robert Bauval and His Influence on Ancient Astronomy
⑤ The Relationship Between the Giza Pyramids and the Constellations

2. Complete the summary by filling in the blanks with the given expressions. Change the form, if necessary.

ancient	position	representation	serve	prominent	claim

One of the most interesting examples of humankind's curiosity about the
constellations can be seen in the _____ Egyptian Pyramids of
Giza. Robert Bauval, a _____ researcher of the pyramids
_____ that the pyramids were designed as part of a master plan to
mirror the layout of the constellations. The pyramids which _____
as Earthly tombs for the dead kings _____ in a way so as to
_____ the specific star that each deceased king became in Sah.

| **Words** | Read the following definitions and find the words in the passage |

- a group of stars which form a pattern and have a name: _____
- the study of planets and their influence on people: _____
- very noticeable: _____
- the way in which the parts of it are arranged: _____
- to say, maintain or assert something: _____
- mutually related or connected: _____
- to place an object in a certain position in relation to something else, usually parallel to it: _____

A. Fill in the blanks with the appropriate words.

| align | contend | entertain | predecessor |

1. You must _____ all three pieces perfectly for the door to open.

2. James felt stressed because his _____ had done such a wonderful job.

3. Guilty or not, most suspects will _____ that they are innocent until the end.

4. There was a live band at the party to _____ the guests.

B. Fill in the blanks with the appropriate expressions.

1. The job was pretty satisfactory **in terms** _____ payment. (= concerning)

2. If you don't **adhere** _____ these rules, you will be disqualified. (= follow)

3. He will **put** _____ his wild theory on the Internet. (= propose)

4. The review said that the restaurant was second _____ **none**. (= best)

5. They were always busy trying to **play a** trick _____ each other. (= fool)

C. Complete the sentences with the given words.

| effect | hand | constellation | quality | layout |

1. Studying all night can have a negative _____ on your test the next day.

2. The planet orbits a star in the _____ of Cepheus.

3. John has the upper _____ because he has played the game before.

4. Sue thought the blanket was good _____ , but she didn't like its design.

5. He tried to recall the _____ of the house because the blueprint was missing.

D. Fill in the blanks with the appropriate expressions. Use the given words.

1. The cable _____ (receive) seems to be bad on extremely rainy days.

2. A student asked the painter what his _____ (inspire) for the painting was.

3. Several suggestions were offered for _____ (adopt) during the meeting.

4. His idea showed promise, but its _____ (execute) was a failure.

5. I made one more _____ (modify) to my paper before handing it in.

E. Choose the best word to complete each sentence.

1. That evening, the _____ shone brightly in the clear night sky.
   ① constellations ② conversations ③ coordinates ④ channels

2. It is more difficult for shy people to _____ with others.
   ① convert ② interact ③ experience ④ devote

3. I saw a picture of my father looking _____ like a true mountain man.
   ① prominent ② hilarious ③ robust ④ adorable

4. The small but important changes made a _____ difference.
   ① ridiculous ② tedious ③ translucent ④ substantial

5. The author's new book _____ his concerns about the environment.
   ① requires ② reflects ③ serves ④ disperses

Identifying the Main Idea and the Title

What is a main idea?

- The main idea is the "key concept" being expressed in the writing.

What is a title?

- The title is the distinguishing name of a writing based on its theme.

Why is it important to identify the main idea and title?

- Most instructors design their tests related to the title and main ideas.

How to solve

- Identifying the main idea

  ⇒ Find out whether there is a clear main idea given in the writing.

  ① It is usually given in the beginning or at the end.

  ② It is usually more "general" than the other sentences. Plurals and the words "many," "numerous," or "several" often signal a thesis sentence.

  ⇒ If not, get information from the following:

  ① repetitive words or expressions

  ② the point of given examples

- Identifying the title

  ① Find the thesis.

  ② Find a keyword if the thesis is not explicit.

  ③ Find an expression similar to keywords used in the thesis.

Find the main idea of the paragraph.

There is healing power in flowers, trees, fresh air and sweet-smelling soil. Just walking through a garden or, for that matter, seeing one out your window, can lower blood pressure, reduce stress, and ease pain. Get out there and start digging, and the benefits multiply. While it may be basic and even old-fashioned, using gardening as a health care tool is blossoming. New or remodeled hospitals and nursing homes increasingly come equipped with healing gardens where patients and staff can get away from barren, indoor surroundings. Many also offer patients a chance to get their hands dirty and their minds engaged in caring for plants.

step 1. Find the topic sentence that contains the main idea of the paragraph.

_____

_____

step 2. Write the supporting ideas.

_____

_____

step 3. Choose the best main idea from the given choices.

① ways of growing flowers   ② curing high blood pressure

③ the healing effects of gardening   ④ conditions for nursing homes

⑤ trends in constructing hospitals

The most incomprehensible thing about science is that it is comprehensible.
- Albert Einstein

Unit 2

Identifying Corresponding / Supporting Details

Read the following and answer the questions.

Imagine you were afraid to leave your own house. What if social problems such as pressure from school or an inability to talk to your family caused you to retreat into your home and live like a hermit? If you've ever felt like hiding from the entire world then you probably understand how many Japanese youngsters are feeling.

Many young Japanese people have retreated into isolation. The increase of this behavior is a real problem in Japanese society. Some reports claim that almost one million Japanese young people are now living a solitary lifestyle.

The "hikikomori" condition can be defined as a form of agoraphobia. Agoraphobia is the fear of being in public places, where one is more likely to experience anxiety or panic; therefore, people with agoraphobia tend not to go out in public. Is there any treatment people with agoraphobia can rely on to overcome their fear?

According to experts, the solution is either medicine, therapy, or a combination of the two. Unfortunately, in Japan, people seem to be scared to <u>address</u> this growing problem. Many families just look the other way as their children withdraw from society, hoping it is just a phase. Hopefully, Japan will give more attention to treating these people who are living their lives in solitude.

Words
Read the following definitions and translate them into Korean.

- **pressure:** stress caused by problems in one's life _____
- **retreat:** to move backwards or away from something _____
- **isolation:** removing oneself from other people _____
- **solitary:** being alone _____
- **panic:** an extreme state of worrying _____
- **address:** to deal with or discuss _____
- **phase:** a certain period or time (in one's life) _____

Impact reading

1. Which is NOT mentioned in the passage?

① Symptoms of the "hikikomori" condition
② Definition of the "hikikomori" condition
③ How the "hikikomori" condition can be prevented
④ Why the "hikikomori" condition in Japan is aggravated
⑤ The number of Japanese youth staying home with no social interaction

2. Which is the closest in meaning to the underlined part?

① How can I address you?
② Jenny addressed the issue.
③ Could you give me your address?
④ Mr. Johnson told his employees to address him by his first name.
⑤ A large parcel was addressed to the personnel department.

3. Write T if the sentence is true. Write F if it is false.

① In Japan, people living in isolation have become a great concern to society. _____
② Some families tend not to take agoraphobia seriously. _____
③ The number of people with agoraphobia is on the decrease due to the development of its therapy. _____

TIP

Akihabara Massacre

+ Akihabara is a major shopping area of Tokyo where you can buy electronics, games and comics. On June 8, 2008, a young man attacked more than a dozen people with a truck and knives, and killed seven of them there. The perpetrator was a temporary worker in a factory and thought himself to be an outcast. It was considered that he committed this terrible crime due to his desperation and loneliness.

Read the following and answer the questions.

With the economic growth of the Asian Pacific region, more people are starting to pay attention to India. For years India's economy remained weak despite the size of both their nation and population. These days, India's economy is growing rapidly at a rate of 9.4% in 2007, and they're quickly becoming an economic superpower.

For years, India wasn't involved in world economics because they wanted to preserve their own economy. However, recent economic and political changes have helped open up India's economy to the world. India's economy is now the 12th strongest in the world, making it one of the most powerful nations in the Asian Pacific region.

How can this be possible considering most of India's wealth still comes from agriculture? A lot of foreign companies are outsourcing their technology industries to India because of the low cost of doing business and the abundance of technical experts.

India's population also plays a large role in the strength of their economy. India's middle-class population is 300 million, which exceeds the population of the United States and the European Union. This number represents _____ because they have a lot of money to spend. If you go to the middle-class areas in Mumbai, you'll find people shopping for luxurious international brands such as Gucci or Ralph Lauren.

As one of the fastest growing economies in the world, India has positioned itself to be a major economic power in the coming years.

Words   Read the following definitions and translate them into Korean.

- **preserve**: to maintain something _____
- **outsource**: to send business out of one's own country to another country _____
- **exceed**: to be larger than a certain amount or number _____
- **luxurious**: high-quality and expensive _____

Impact reading

1. Which is NOT true according to the passage?

① India's population plays a positive role in the economy.

② India's advanced technology contributes to their economy.

③ India is outsourcing their technology to foreign countries.

④ India is getting more attention as a growing economic power.

⑤ In the past, the economic potential of India was underestimated.

2. What is the most appropriate for the blank?

① a powerful consumer market

② more savings as a whole country

③ a large number of the population

④ more tax influx to the government

⑤ a strong need to regulate population

3. Match the main idea with each paragraph.

Paragraph 2 •   • India's middle class is playing a major role
                       in creating a good economy.

Paragraph 3 •   • India's recent changes have helped to improve
                       their economy.

Paragraph 4 •   • India has become involved in many industries
                       besides agriculture.

 TIP

Languages in India

✦ Many countries have more than one official language. In India, Hindi and English
are considered as official languages. However, there are hundreds of languages
and thousands of dialects. 29 languages are spoken by more than a million
people. The Indian government recognizes 22 official regional languages, spoken
in different parts of the country.

If you grew up in North America, chances are you used to papier-mâché as a child. However, to others around the world this strange sounding concept is unknown. Let's shed some light on this fun and easy art form.

Papier-mâché gets its name from the French words meaning 'chewed-up paper'. Essentially, papier-mâché is the process of creating a 3-dimensional object by applying pieces of paper soaked in a wet paste to a frame.

Many children use papier-mâché in art class to make things like colorful pinatas (animals or shapes which are filled with candy and then broken apart by children hitting them with a stick), exotic animals, and dramatic masks. It can be a pretty sticky process and the artist usually ends up covered in paste as well, however, that is exactly what makes papier-mâché so fun for children. For those who don't mind getting their hands dirty, papier-mâché can be done by following these steps.

First, prepare some wet paste by mixing glue or starch with water. Second, gather pieces of paper or newspaper, rip them into small pieces and soak them in the paste. Third, create a frame for whatever you want to make (often something as simple as a

balloon will do the trick) and cover it with the paste-soaked bits of paper. Next, the paper dries, becoming hard and strong. Once it has dried, the frame can be removed and we are left with the papier-mâché creation. Finally, the artist can paint their creation or decorate it by adding colorful paper and ribbons.

If you've never had the experience of papier-mâché then hopefully this will inspire you to follow the above steps to make your own papier-mâché art. It may be sticky and messy, but it is also a lot of fun!

TIP

Barbie Dolls

+ Around the world, many girls played with Barbie in their childhood, but few of them really know Barbie. In the 1950's. Barbie's creator, Ruth Handler saw her daughter Barbara playing with paper dolls and got the idea for Barbie. At that time, most dolls had child-like appearances. She thought about creating an independent adult doll in her mind. Ironically, today Barbie is often criticized for giving girls the wrong idea for a woman's ideal body.

Impact reading

1. Which is NOT mentioned in the passage?

① When papier-mâché first began
② How to make paste for papier-mâché
③ The origin of the word "papier-mâché"
④ The process to make papier-mâché artwork
⑤ The popularity of papier-mâché in North America

2. Which can NOT be inferred from the passage?

① Papier-mâché is messy.
② Papier-mâché is complicated.
③ Papier-mâché is popular in North America.
④ Papier-mâché is a fun way to create artwork.
⑤ Papier-mâché creations can be 3-dimensional.

3. Which of the following steps is NOT related to papier-mâché?

① Mix some glue or starch with water.
② Put some small pieces of paper into paste.
③ Make the desired frame with sticky paper.
④ Cover the frame with the paste-soaked paper.
⑤ Dry the form and remove the original frame.

Words	Read the following definitions and translate them into Korean.

• **concept**: idea or abstract principle _____
• **chewed-up**: bitten up _____
• **3-dimensional**: just like reality, the measurement such as length, width, or height _____
• **frame**: the wood, metal, or plastic that is fitted around it _____
• **exotic**: unusual and interesting, usually because it is related to a distant country _____
• **starch**: substance that is found in foods such as bread, potatoes, and rice_____

Read the following and answer the questions.

Have you ever looked into the night sky and wondered how stars are created? Actually, these beautiful balls of light began as a cloud of gas and dust many light-years ago. Once enough gas and dust have been pulled into a giant ball as a result of gravitational force, the center reaches a temperature of 15 million degrees. (a) At this stage a wondrous event occurs; a new star has begun its life in our universe.

Most of a star's life is spent burning hydrogen in its core, converting it into heat and light. (b) Depending on the star's size, it will run out of this fuel after several million or billion years. (c) This causes the outer layers of the star collapsing inward, increasing the temperature and pressure once again. New heat is created and temporarily counteracts gravity, (d) expanding the outer layers of the star to enormous proportions. This is called the "red giant" stage.

The final fate of a star depends on its initial mass. A low or medium mass star's outer layers continue to expand while the core contracts inward. Helium atoms in the core fuse together to form carbon. With no fuel left to burn, the star spends the rest of its days cooling and shrinking. This cold dark star is called a black dwarf.

Massive stars have more fuel in their core, (e) which starts to shrink, growing hotter and denser until it explodes in one of the most spectacular events in the Universe. The shock propels the material away from the star in a tremendous explosion called a supernova.

After a star reaches the phase of black dwarf or supernova, it remains an enormous cloud of dust, until gravity pulls it together and the cycle begins again.

1. Which is the best title for the passage?

① How Stars Are Born
② Two Different Fates of a Star
③ Supernova: The Birth of a Star
④ A Wondrous Event: Birth of Stars
⑤ The Life Cycles and Stages of Stars

Impact reading

2. Which is true according to the passage?

① A massive star becomes a red giant.
② Low or medium mass stars become supernovae.
③ The heat and light of a star comes from burning oxygen.
④ Gravity pulls an enormous cloud of gas and dust together.
⑤ Low or medium mass stars' outer layers continue to contract.

3. Which of the underlined parts is NOT grammatically correct?

① (a)
② (b)
③ (c)
④ (d)
⑤ (e)

| Words | Read the following definitions and find the words in the passage. |

- relating to or resulting from the force of gravity: _____
- to change into a different form: _____
- to reduce its effect by doing something that produces an opposite effect: _____
- happening at the beginning of a process: _____
- to become smaller or shorter: _____
- to join together physically or chemically, usually to become one thing: _____
- to force to do something: _____

Read the following and answer the questions.

When we arrived at Pompeii, we realized that the whole city was so well preserved by the volcanic eruption that it made it easy to imagine life back in 100 B.C. We could easily see that the civilization of Pompeii was incredibly advanced.

We also found out a few interesting points about Pompeii while exploring the city. During the disaster the main killer was not lava, as we had thought, but rather the poisonous gases and ash clouds spewed by the volcano in the sudden eruption. And, unlike popular belief that all of the inhabitants of Pompeii died that day, the population of Pompeii is estimated to have been reduced dramatically due to a huge earthquake prior to the eruption.

Another amazing sight were the preserved bodies. There were people in all sorts of painful looking positions. You can just imagine them trying to run from the volcano or trying to hide their faces. It was pretty creepy. We heard that when excavation began, a worker found a cavity in the hardened ash with bones at the bottom. A scientist had the ingenious idea of pouring plaster into the cavity in the rock and then chipping away the rock from around the hardened plaster. What remained was an exact copy of the person who was killed in the exact position he or she was in when they were overcome by the ash.

We had a great time wandering through the ruined houses and villas and exploring this amazing city. We were fascinated by the way the city was frozen in time as well as the many interesting things we learned on our trip. Heading back to the hotel along the Amalfi coast, we were pretty tired but we were excited about our experience here in Pompeii.

Words

Read the following definitions and find the words in the passage.

- relating to or produced by a volcano or volcanoes: _____
- breaking out suddenly and violently: _____
- to judge or calculate (size or amount, etc.) roughly or without measuring: _____
- slightly scary; spooky: _____
- an act of digging up or uncovering something: _____
- showing or having skills, originality and inventive cleverness: _____
- to walk, move or travel about, with no particular destination; to ramble: _____

1. What style of writing is this?

① Book Review
② Travel Journal
③ Autobiography
④ Newspaper Article
⑤ Abstract of a Paper

Impact reading

2. Which is true about the passage?

① Architectural skills were undeveloped in Pompeii.
② All the people in Pompeii died from a volcanic disaster.
③ It is believed an earthquake contributed to the destruction of Pompeii.
④ The lava from the volcano was the main killer of people in Pompeii.
⑤ People in Pompeii were restored by sculptors for historical record.

3. Complete the summary by filling in the blanks with the given expressions. Change the form, if necessary.

volcano	exemplify	remains	bustle	wipe out

Visitors to Pompeii will be amazed by the well-preserved _____ of this city. They will also be surprised to learn that the historic _____ eruption may not have been solely responsible for _____ this civilization. The eerie sleeplike state of this once _____ place realistically _____ life back in 100 B.C.

A. Fill in the blanks with the appropriate words.

| address | concept | consumer | ingenious | initial |

1. One student came up with an _____ way to cut watermelons.

2. The new products were a big hit because they met _____ needs.

3. The committee decided to wait and _____ the issue at the next meeting.

4. The _____ of beauty has continued to change throughout history.

5. The _____ stock in the cellar had twenty cases of red wine.

B. Connect each expression in column A with the matching expression in column B.

A	B
1. look the other way •	• to make something clear
2. live like a hermit •	• to ignore something wrong or unpleasant
3. shine light on •	• to slowly break pieces off something
4. run out of •	• to live apart from the rest of society
5. chip away •	• to use up the last of something

C. Fill in the blanks with the appropriate expressions.

1. Our team lost the game _____ **a result of** Bill's own goal. (= because of)

2. The Internet has **opened** _____ a whole new way of communicating. (= made available)

3. I'm afraid I'll _____ **up** eating the whole cake by myself. (= finally doing)

4. My mom **played a** big _____ in my dad's success. (= perform a function)

5. We **were** _____ **by** shock watching the news. (= unable to move due to)

D. Fill in the blanks with the appropriate expressions. Use the given words.

1. It was my first time being a part of a _____ (drama) performance.

2. The black mamba's _____ (poison) venom can even bring down a lion.

3. The patient will be kept in _____ (isolate) until the test results come out.

4. Their _____ (luxury) house had ten bedrooms and a swimming pool.

5. Many famous archaeologists will take part in this _____ (excavate).

E. Choose the best word to complete each sentence.

1. The officer told his men to _____ into the forest and take cover.
   ① erupt   ② expand   ③ retreat   ④ remove

2. He felt the _____ to improve his failing math grades.
   ① proportion   ② solitude   ③ attention   ④ pressure

3. My dad plans to _____ small room into a home-theatre room.
   ① convert   ② collapse   ③ propel   ④ explode

4. I could feel the force of _____ pulling us down to the ground.
   ① aviation   ② gravity   ③ starch   ④ civilization

5. The _____ characters seemed to pop out of the screen.
   ① three-dimensional   ② well-preserved   ③ light-years   ④ paste-soaked

Identifying Corresponding / Supporting Details

▍ What is identifying correspondence?

Identifying correspondence is the process of figuring out whether specific expressions can be inferred from the passage or not.

▍ What are supporting details?

While the main idea tells the reader what the "key concept" is, the supporting details give facts and ideas that support the main idea.

▍ Why are they important?

Many reading comprehension questions ask readers to find supporting details that can be inferred from the writing or not. In order to answer this type of question, readers need to be able to grasp the main idea of a passage as wells as identify its supporting details.

▍ How to solve

- Identifying correspondence

  ① Read the choices first.
    In most cases, the order of the given choices corresponds with the order they appear in the writing.
  ② Study antonyms and idiomatic expressions.
    The choices may paraphrase the expressions used in the writing.
  ③ Do not entirely rely on one's common sense.

- Identifying supporting details

  ① Identify the purpose of the passage.
  ② Pay attention to the transition words used in the passage.

Actual Test

Read the passage and answer the following questions.

> Recreational tree climbing is an evolving sport. It got its start in 1983, when Peter Jenkins began teaching all sorts of people, including children, how to climb trees safely using a rope and a harness and the recreational tree climbing technique. In the United States, it is now practiced by a thousand or so people but is rapidly growing in popularity. However, those who study rare plants are worried about recreational tree climbers. They fear that these climbers may try to climb the biggest and tallest trees if they learn their exact locations. Any contact between humans and rare plants can be disastrous for the plants.

step 1. Write the first word of the second part when the writing is divided into two parts.

_____

step 2. Fill in the blanks with words in the passage.

These days recreational tree climbing is growing in _____ ,
but it can be _____ for the plants.

step 3. What cannot be inferred from the writing about recreational tree climbing?

① Peter Jenkins started instructing in 1983.
② Children were also educated to climb in a safe manner.
③ It is becoming famous in the States.
④ People who research rare plants enjoy climbing.
⑤ The contact between people and rare plants can threaten the plants.

Only the unreasonable man persists in trying to adapt the world to himself.
Therefore, all progress depends on the unreasonable man.
- George Bernard Shaw

Unit 3

Grasping the Logical Flow

Read the following and answer the questions.

Did you know that energy can be generated from food, or more specifically, the chemicals found in food? You can create a chemical reaction with the acid of a lemon and metal which will produce enough energy to power a small light. Creating a battery from a lemon is a common project in many science textbooks, and is popular at science fairs.

The lemon battery is a voltaic battery, which converts chemical energy into electrical energy. It is made up of two different metals: copper and zinc. You can easily find copper at hardware stores, but alternatively, you can also use a copper penny that was made before 1982 (pennies made after 1982 contain less copper).

Electric current enters and exits the battery through these metals using the acid from the lemon, a solution which can conduct electricity. (a)_____, the more lemons you have, the more energy you will create. A chemical reaction takes place between the acid and the metal which produces electrons, the main component of energy. Enough energy is created to cause the LED light to light up.

It is an easy experiment that you can try at home with your family. If you want to learn more, why not try using different fruits (b)_____ a lemon and see what happens?

Words   Read the following definitions and translate them into Korean.

• **generate**: to produce or create something _____

• **voltaic battery**: a non-rechargeable cell or battery that produces an electric current by chemical reactions

_____

• **contain**: to consist of, or hold something _____

• **acid**: any of a group of compounds that have a sour or sharp taste _____

• **reaction**: action or change in the chemical process _____

• **electron**: a particle which has a negative electric charge and is responsible for carrying electricity

_____

Impact reading

1. Which is most likely to follow the passage?

① how to make a lemon battery

② using other acidic fruits to create energy

③ an experiment using other metals and lemons

④ making a LED signboard with a lemon battery

⑤ how to check acidity levels in lemons used to create electricity

2. What are the most appropriate expressions for blanks (a) and (b)?

	(a)	(b)
①	On the other hand	as well as
②	Therefore	except for
③	Likewise	along with
④	Consequently	in addition to
⑤	Therefore	in place of

3. Write T if the statement is true. Write F if it is false.

① Copper pennies made after 1982 are useful to generate energy. _____

② The acidity of fruit creates a chemical reaction by itself. _____

③ Copper content is important to the success of this experiment. _____

TIP

Frozen to Death or Not?

✦ What would you do if you were diagnosed with a terminal disease? Would you just give up? Some people take a risk with the possibility that the cure will be found in the future. Instead of accepting their coming death, they choose to be preserved at a low temperature. However, it is currently impossible to revive these people.

Read the following and answer the questions.

Did you know that earthworms determine how healthy soil is? The value of an earthworm is more than just fish bait or a snack for birds! It is known that the structure and fertility of garden soil are in the care of the lowly earthworm. (A)

Why is this the case? Earthworms benefit the soil in two ways. First, they improve soil through tunneling. Earthworms eat their way through the earth and the resulting maze of tunnels allows water and air to penetrate the soil. By building these porous networks, earthworms promote efficient water and nutrient cycling for the plants to use. (B)

The other way earthworms improve soil is through their feeding. Feeding is accomplished at the same time as tunneling. (C) As the earthworm passes through the soil, it eats, deposits castings and neutralizes the soil by secreting calcium carbonate from glands near its gizzard. (D) Earthworm activities directly stimulate organisms that trap, eat, and out-compete plant-eating parasites. (E)

Then how many earthworms are necessary for healthy soil? According to the United States Department of Agriculture Information, an acre of land can host up to 500,000 earthworms. Having as many earthworms as possible seems to work better than any other natural or artificial fertilizers for growing plants.

| Words | Read the following definitions and translate them into Korean. |

- **bait**: something that is put on a hook in order to catch fish _____
- **fertility**: ability to support the growth of a large number of healthy plants _____
- **penetrate**: to get into or pass through _____
- **secrete**: to produce something _____
- **fertilizer**: a substance you spread on the ground in order to make plants grow more successfully

_____

Impact reading

1. Where does the following sentence best fit?

In addition to improving soil structure and fertility, research
has found soil rich with earthworms hosts fewer parasites.

① (A)   ② (B)   ③ (C)   ④ (D)   ⑤ (E)

2. Which is NOT true about the passage?

① The castings of earthworms improve soil quality.
② The maze made by earthworms improves soil quality.
③ The digestion process of earthworms makes soil healthier.
④ The porous network made by earthworms is good for plants.
⑤ Earthworms' activities enhance soil quality by nurturing parasites.

3. Match the main idea with each paragraph.

Paragraph 2 •   • The more earthworms that are in the soil, the better the soil quality will be.

Paragraph 3 •   • Earthworms help improve soil quality and control parasites.

Paragraph 4 •   • Earthworms increase the quality of soil by tunneling.

TIP

Ladybugs

+ Ladybugs are little beetles that are usually red with black spots. They look so pretty that they are used in many designs. However, they are not just beautiful insects. Ladybugs are generally considered to be useful insects because they eat aphids, which destroy plants and gardens.

Read the following and answer the questions.

How would you feel about a director who demanded that a stream be made to run in the opposite direction to produce a better visual effect? How about dyeing the rain water black with ink to portray a heavy downpour, while consuming the entire local water supply? You might think him or her insane. However, if the director happens to be Akira Kurosawa, it's a totally different story.

Akira Kurosawa (1910-1998) is a world famous Japanese film director, producer, and scriptwriter. He made such famous experimental films as *Rashomon*, *Seven Samurai*, and *Ran*. He received the Golden Lion for *Rashomon* and the Silver Lion for *Seven Samurai* at the Venice Film Festival, and went on to earn an Oscar for *Lifetime Achievement* in 1989. (a) He was well-known for his perfectionism as a director. (b) He poured all his energy into achieving the desired visual effects. (c) He once asked his actors to wear their costumes weeks before the actual shooting, so that the costumes would look worn by the time the filming began. (d) He even went so far as to nearly kill his main actress in a scene, where he used expert archers to shoot real arrows at her. (e) Luckily, the archers were so skilled that the heroine was relieved.

During his lifetime, Akira Kurosawa experienced mad times in Japanese history. He once remarked, "In a mad world, only the mad are sane." He survived being one of the 'mad,' and his films are the very testimony to this fact.

Words   Read the following definitions and translate them into Korean.

- **visual:** relating to sight _____
- **portray:** to depict, play the part of _____
- **perfectionism:** extreme or obsessive striving for perfection _____
- **costume:** a set of clothes worn while performing _____
- **archer:** a person who shoots with a bow and arrow _____
- **sane:** thinking and behaving normally and reasonably _____
- **testimony:** any form of evidence, indication, proof _____

Impact reading

1. Which does not fit in the passage? Choose one from (a) to (e).

① (a)   ② (b)   ③ (c)   ④ (d)   ⑤ (e)

2. Which is NOT mentioned in the passage?

① Awards that Akira Kurosawa won
② Akira Kurosawa's directorial approach
③ Akira Kurosawa's dramatic filmography style
④ Educational background of Akira Kurosawa
⑤ Examples of Akira Kurosawa's perfectionism

3. Which can NOT be inferred from the passage?

① Kurosawa had a reputation for being tenacious.
② Kurosawa was one of the most productive directors.
③ Kurosawa lived through hard times in Japanese history.
④ Kurosawa's films defied the boundaries of normalcy.
⑤ Kurosawa's perfectionism also showed in his approach to costumes.

TIP

Hollywood Loves Japanese Culture

+ Since the 19th century, the exotic Japanese culture has attracted many Westerners. Japanese paintings and antiques experienced quite a boom in Europe. Today, Hollywood has made lots of Japan-influenced films with major stars. Tom Cruise starred in *The Last Samurai* and Uma Thurman played the role of woman who practiced Japanese swordplay to get revenge on her enemies in *Kill Bill*.

Read the following and answer the questions.

What happens to naughty boys and girls who are constantly on the go, as though they are driven by motors? In the past, people believed that these unruly, ill-behaved kids would eventually outgrow their uncontrollable behavior with time. However, recent studies prove the contrary. Chances are high that these overactive kids may have a serious illness related to a brain disorder.

(A) The problem is that people, including parents of ADHD kids, don't fully understand this disease. It is a medical condition which requires proper medical diagnosis and treatment. It is very important, therefore, to recognize that ADHD is treatable once it's diagnosed properly.

(B) Attention-Deficit / Hyperactivity Disorder (more commonly referred to as ADHD) is a neurological brain disorder that affects approximately 5 % of children worldwide. Children with ADHD are known to demonstrate symptoms such as inattention, hyperactivity and impulsivity.

(C) For example, if a child is easily distracted and has trouble paying attention in times of study or play for a period exceeding 6 months, he or she may be diagnosed with ADHD. Children with ADHD display disruptive behavior which causes friction both at home and at school. They tend to have a more difficult time getting along with their friends and may even be rejected by them at school.

The earlier ADHD is diagnosed and treated, the better it will be for kids with ADHD and their parents. Without proper diagnosis, these kids could experience a lifetime of frustration. Even worse, they might not live up to their full potential.

1. Which best describes the writer's opinion?

① ADHD is hard to detect at an early stage.

② The government should support children with ADHD.

③ Parents should know better than to evaluate their children.

④ The importance of early diagnosis of ADHD can't be ignored.

⑤ Children with ADHD should be taught to overcome their difficulties.

Impact reading

2. What is the correct order of this passage?

① (A) − (B) − (C)

② (B) − (A) − (C)

③ (B) − (C) − (A)

④ (C) − (A) − (B)

⑤ (C) − (B) − (A)

3. What symptoms do children with ADHD normally display? Find the words in the passage.

They display _____.

Words	Read the following definitions and find the words in the passage.

• to discover the nature of a disease through various examinations: _____

• a state of being unable to relax: _____

• related to the branch of medicine dealing with the nervous system: _____

• a tendency to act without thinking first: _____

• inattentive: _____

• causing disruption or disturbances: _____

• disagreement, conflict because of differences of opinion: _____

Read the following and answer the questions.

'Freeter' is a Japanese word combining the English word 'free' and the German word 'arbeiter (laborer).' Some also say 'Freeter' is a shortened expression for 'Free timer.' Whatever its origin, the term 'Freeter' refers to the group of young people who have one or more part-time jobs or move from one short-term job to another without having a full-time job.

(A) In 2002, the number of Freeters reached 2 million in Japan. The Freeter lifestyle is different from most people in their thirties, who usually enter a career and get married during this period of life. Many Freeters are unmarried, and some of them are economically dependent on their parents, leading a 'parasitic' life.

Why do Japanese young people choose to become Freeters, giving up a stable and secure lifestyle? It is often considered to be a result of the unemployment problem in Japan. In 2000, only 55.8% of college graduates managed to get a job, due to a lack of jobs for young people. (B) But another reason Freeters say that they deliberately chose this lifestyle is in order to pursue their dreams. To have more free time, they would rather have several part-time jobs instead of being tied up at one company all day long.

(C) Freeters are creating new social issues in Japan. Those who live a parasitic life by depending on their parents financially are often blamed for the decrease in birth rate and the increase in crime. (D) When asked what they think about Freeters, 48% of non-Freeters replied that they could understand people becoming Freeters and only 28% of respondents said they could not understand. (E) Freeters (including parasite singles) may not have any other option in the current difficult economic situation in Japan.

| Words | Read the following definitions and find the words in the passage. |

- needing someone else (like parents) in order to survive: _____
- not likely to change or come to an end suddenly: _____
- safe from harm or attack: _____
- intentionally, by design: _____
- to carry or follow: _____
- a person who replies to something such as a survey or question: _____
- a small animal or plant that lives on or inside a larger animal: _____
- happening at the present time: _____

1. Which is NOT true about the passage?

① People become Freeters as a result of the economy.

② People become Freeters because they can't find a job.

③ People become Freeters in order to pursue their dreams.

④ People become Freeters because they want more free time.

⑤ People become Freeters because they want to get married
   and have a career.

Impact reading

2. Where does the following sentence best fit?

However, according to recent survey results,
people seem to understand and sympathize with Freeters.

① (A)   ② (B)   ③ (C)   ④ (D)   ⑤ (E)

3. Complete the summary by filling in the blanks with the given
   expressions. Change the form, if necessary.

employment   career   evitable   sympathize   follow

Freeters don't have _____ jobs because they prefer to
have a few part-time jobs due to _____ or because they
want more free time to _____ their dreams. Some people
blame Freeters for social problems. On the other hand, most people
_____ with them as they think it is an _____
phenomenon resulting from a bad economic situation.

A. Fill in the blanks with the appropriate words.

> | fertilizer | reaction | sane | stable | unruly |

1. The teacher got angry and told us that we were a very _____ class.
2. John finally landed a _____ job working as a car salesman.
3. Studies show that some patients had a bad _____ to the medicine.
4. The farmer tried using a different kind of manure as his _____.
5. Although she was mentally ill, she looked quite _____ when she was quiet.

B. Match the underlined phrases with their meanings.

> a. be busy at   b. fulfill   c. consists of   d. concentrate on   e. as well as

1. I expect you to live up to the terms of our agreement. _____
2. She can't make it because she is tied up at the office. _____
3. The structure is made up of toothpicks glued together. _____
4. In addition to owning two cars, he owns a motorcycle. _____
5. Let's pour all our energy into getting this project done. _____

C. Fill in the blanks with the appropriate expressions.

1. He will **be in the** _____ of a 24-hour bodyguard. (= be protected by)
2. They say he _____ **up** a brilliant career in medicine. (= stopped trying for)
3. There were holes in the photo **in** _____ **of** her ex-boyfriend. (= instead of)
4. Business was booming and he was always **on the** _____. (= constantly active)
5. He **wore** _____ his running shoes practicing for the race. (= used until damaged)

D. Fill in the blanks with the appropriate expressions. Use the given words.

1. There is a new drug, but it is still at the _____ (experiment) stage.

2. The roads were built with _____ (pore) materials to prevent flooding.

3. Some children's _____ (impulsive) can lead them to act unruly.

4. The construction noise was so _____ (disrupt) that the meeting was cut short.

5. Having four _____ (depend) children left her with hardly any spare time.

E. Choose the best word to complete each sentence.

1. A simple device can _____ enough energy to light a light bulb.
   ① observe   ② generate   ③ neutralize   ④ portray

2. After several minutes, the thick oil began to _____ the cloth surface.
   ① demand   ② diagnose   ③ penetrate   ④ deposit

3. Just thinking about giving his _____ in court made his stomach turn.
   ① testimony   ② friction   ③ disorder   ④ gizzard

4. Since the problem isn't _____, you won't need brain surgery.
   ① voltaic   ② visual   ③ neurological   ④ electrical

5. I needed to find one more _____ to finish my opinion poll.
   ① bait   ② archer   ③ electron   ④ respondent

Grasping the Logical Flow

Why do we need to grasp the logical flow?

In order to write well, it is important to be able to explain a certain topic in a logical manner.

Reading comprehension questions in textbooks or exams ask readers to find sentences that are inconsistent with the writing or to put a sentence in the most appropriate place.

How to solve

- Finding sentences inconsistent with the writing

  ① Identify the main idea and figure out whether the flow of the writing is consistent based on its main idea.

  ② Identify a sentence that disturbs the flow of the writing.

  ③ Even a sentence that repeats a word related to the main idea can be inconsistent with the writing.

- Putting sentences in adequate places

  ① Grasp the overall flow of the writing.

  ② Use transition words and directives as clues.

  ③ Judge whether the given sentence is the topic sentence or supporting sentence.

  ④ Focus on transition words because they are important.

Actual Test

Read the passage and answer the following questions.

When one group borrows something such as ideas, values, foods, or styles of architecture from another group, change occurs through diffusion. ① Diffusion is a process by which one culture or society borrows from another. ② The extent and rate of diffusion depend on the degree of social contact. ③ The more contact a group has with another group, the more likely it is that objects or ideas will be exchanged. ④ The exclusion of new technology generally leads to social change that will soon follow. ⑤ Social contact, therefore, plays a crucial role in the process of diffusion.

step 1. Find the sentence that expresses the definition of 'diffusion.'

_____

step 2. Write T if the statement is true and F if it is false.

① The speed of diffusion decreases as there is more social contact between cultures. _____

② Not only tangible assets but also intangible assets such as values and ideologies can be diffused. _____

step 3. Find a sentence that is inconsistent with the overall flow of the paragraph.

①   ②   ③   ④   ⑤

Only the unreasonable man persists in trying to adapt the world to himself.
Therefore, all progress depends on the unreasonable man.
- George Bernard Shaw

Unit 4

Making Inferences

Read the following and answer the questions.

Have you ever decided to spend an afternoon at home with a cup of coffee and a good book, only to discover that you're out of coffee or you've read everything on your bookshelf? No problem! _____ can provide all the comforts of home, plus some added extras.

If you're in the mood for a good read, just choose one of many books or magazines and make yourself at home in one of the cozy chairs. The lighting is easy on the eyes, so you can read as long as you want without getting a headache. If you're not much of a reader, wireless internet is also available.

If it's a good cup of coffee you're after, there are many to choose from. Free toast is also provided! The fresh brewed coffee is refillable and delicious. The menu also offers light meals such as sandwiches and waffles.

In addition to the comforts of home, this cafe offers something unusual: doctor fish. These tiny fish eat away the dead skin from your feet and promote blood circulation. It's an interesting pedicure if you can handle having your feet tickled. Doctor fish are a popular attraction at the cafe, so you may have to wait.

So next time you feel like relaxing, see if there is a cafe like this in your neighborhood. These total entertainment cafes unite the best features of a coffee shop, internet cafe and health spa into one comfortable space.

| Words | Read the following definitions and translate them into Korean. |

- **wireless**: having no wire _____
- **refillable**: able to fill again _____
- **pedicure**: professional care and treatment of the feet _____

Impact reading

1. Which can NOT be inferred from the passage?

① People can enjoy free Internet service.

② People can stay there as long as they want.

③ This facility was originally designed as a pedicure spa.

④ This cafe has introduced a new concept to cafe.

⑤ People can read books while enjoying the comfortable atmosphere.

2. What is the most appropriate expression for the blank?

① A traditional bookstore

② A wide variety of books

③ A new hybrid cafe-bookstore

④ A new medical care system

⑤ An unusual foot massage

3. Write T if the sentence is true. Write F it is false.

① This new cafe provides a variety of services. _____

② It is proven doctor fish have special medical benefits. _____

③ Free meals are provided for people who want to enjoy a foot bath. _____

TIP

The New Trend of Foot Baths

✦ After long hours of standing and walking with high heels on, you will surely need some rest for your tired feet. Especially on hot and humid summer days, your sweaty and foul smelling feet will definitely love some hours of relaxation. Besides, you need to keep your feet clean and dry in order to avoid fungal infections. By visiting a 'foot bath' cafe, you can easily satisfy what your feet desperately need. What's more, it relieves stress and fatigue.

Read the following and answer the questions.

Have you ever just wanted to stay home from school? Of course! Whether it's to avoid a test, or to spend the day playing computer games, (a) <u>every student has experienced the urge to skip school</u> at some point. For most children this happens only once in a while, but, for some kids, it's a daily occurrence. These few have a phobia of going to school. But why are they so afraid?

(b) <u>School phobia has many contributing factors.</u> Some children simply feel homesick, while others find the social and/or academic pressures associated with school too much to bear. Bullying or teasing by other students can also be the root cause, as can problems within the home itself, such as a recent divorce or illness. In some cases, a learning disability can create extra pressure in the classroom environment. (c) <u>Alone or compiling, these factors cause anxiety</u> which results in the child's refusal to attend school. In fact, about 5% of children experience school phobia as a result of these, and other issues.

Children who dread going to school will constantly make up reasons not to attend, such as a stomachache or a headache. These students often miss a lot of school, (d) <u>making keeping up with the rest of their class problematic.</u> So how can school phobia be cured?

It's important to find the source of the child's anxiety, and alert the school and teachers to the problem so that they can be more understanding. Often a child may not know why he or she is school-phobic. It's crucial that parents, teachers and, if needed, a child psychologist, (e) <u>work together to help the child adjust and feel more comfortable</u> within the school environment.

Words	Read the following definitions and translate them into Korean.

- **contributing:** adding to the cause of something _____
- **compile:** to combine, to put together _____
- **dread:** to fear something _____
- **constantly:** all the time _____
- **problematic:** troublesome, causing a problem _____
- **crucial:** of extreme importance _____

Impact reading

1. Which can be inferred from the passage?

① Students have to consult a psychologist regularly.
② Parents should help teachers to control school phobia.
③ There may be multiple factors leading to school phobia.
④ School-phobic students need more attention from other students.
⑤ The number of school-phobic students has been on the increase.

2. Which is NOT grammatically correct? Choose one from (a) to (e).

① (a)　　　② (b)　　　③ (c)　　　④ (d)　　　⑤ (e)

3. Match the main idea with each paragraph.

Paragraph 1 •　　　• There are a variety of things that can cause school phobia.

Paragraph 2 •　　　• The cooperation of parents, teachers, and psychologists is necessary to help school-phobic children.

Paragraph 3 •　　　• School-phobic kids tend to fall behind in their studies.

Paragraph 4 •　　　• Some students suffer from the symptom of being afraid of going to school.

TIP

Xenophobia

✦ Are you shy of strangers? It is a kind of the natural self-protection instinct. However, some people have unreasonable fear or hatred of foreign people. It is called xenophobia, originating from the Greek words xeno(foreigner) and phobos(fear). In many cases, xenophobia and racism seem to have similar meaning.

Read the following and answer the questions.

The American government has made a felony crime of intentional, negligent, or reckless abandonment of any animal that is in a person's custody. Animal abandonment is when a person leaves a domesticated animal somewhere without providing for the continued care of that animal. It can often result in serious injury, illness, or even the death of the animal. Every year 8-12 million animals enter shelters. Of that number 5-9 million are euthanized.

Judy: _____

_____. When pets are abandoned, they can contract deadly diseases such as rabies and then there's no choice but euthanasia. I think that all life should be respected.

Wyllie: _____

_____. Laws are supposed to protect people, not animals. My girlfriend used to spend an extravagant amount of money raising her cat. I've even heard of people leaving money to cats in their will. I think it should be a crime that some people spend such a crazy amount of money on animals instead of spending it on people.

Melanie: _____

_____

_____.

I heard on the news the other day that the disease SARS can be passed on by pet cats. If we abandon our pets, it could become a pandemic! Who knows how many diseases they could spread?

| Words | Read the following definitions and translate them into Korean. |

- **felony:** a very serious crime _____
- **abandonment:** an act of leaving something alone _____
- **custody:** the legal right or duty to take care of something _____
- **extravagant:** way too much _____
- **pandemic:** a worldwide sickness _____

Impact reading

1. Which sentence best fits each person's opinion of animal abandonment?

(a) I don't agree that animal abandonment should be considered a crime.

(b) I can't believe that someone would actually throw their pet away like a piece of trash.

(c) The abandonment of animals is not only illegal, it is also dangerous to our health and ecologically destructive.

Judy: _____

Wyllie: _____

Melanie: _____

2. Which is NOT true according to the passage?

① Wyllie thinks spending too much money on pets is unreasonable.

② Melanie worries about other consequences of abandoning animals.

③ Melanie thinks all contagious diseases come from abandoned pets.

④ Judy strongly supports the policy making animal abandonment illegal.

⑤ Wyllie disagrees with the idea of cracking down on pet abandonment.

3. What is the closest in meaning to the underlined part "spread" in the last paragraph? Find the expression in the passage.

_____

TIP

How to Care for Your Pet

✦ Pets are now part of our world. A lot of people love them and live with them. To live together, pet owners should take responsibility for their pets. When you have a pet, you should consider whether to have your pet neutered or not. Some people think neutering is a violation of animal rights. However, neutering your pet not only prevents pet overpopulation, but also improves your pet's health.

Read the following and answer the questions.

Imagine you are standing in a pool of water beneath a fruit tree with low branches. Whenever you reach for a piece of fruit, the branch raises it from your grasp, and when you bend down to get a drink, the water recedes before you can get even a drop. Feel tantalized? The word "tantalize" comes from the Greek myth about Tantalus.

Tantalus, who was uniquely favored among mortals, was invited to Zeus' table in Olympus. There he stole the food of the gods, ambrosia, and brought it back to his people. He also revealed the secrets of the gods, and that wasn't all! He even killed his own son, as a sacrifice to the gods. He cooked his son and tried to serve the meat to the gods to see if they truly did know all. The gods were aware of his intention and refused to accept his sacrifice. However, the goddess, Demeter unknowingly ate some of it. For all his crimes, Tantalus was punished by being perpetually "tantalized" by hunger and thirst in the Underworld.

You might think the punishment for Tantalus was too harsh, but most will agree that his immoral behavior had to be condemned in some way. As we can see from the story of Tantalus, myths teach us about moral behavior through examples. Through

mythology we can also look into the psyche of past cultures. Mythology can teach us what was important in different cultures, as well as how people related to each other. We can also see that ancient cultures struggled with the same issues that we do today. Even the word tantalize, meaning "to tempt," represents one of mankind's eternal struggles.

1. What is the main purpose of this passage?

    ① To signify the function of mythology
    ② To criticize a cruel Greek punishment
    ③ To introduce the mythological figure, Tantalus
    ④ To tell two different meanings of the word 'tantalize'
    ⑤ To explain the history and meaning of the word 'tantalize'

2. What is the best definition of the word "tantalizing" as inferred from the passage?

    ① Hope for a bright future
    ② A desire for eternal life
    ③ A feeling of satisfaction
    ④ An attraction to great success
    ⑤ Temptation without satisfaction

Impact reading

3. Which can be inferred from the passage?

    ① Tantalus killed his daughter.
    ② Tantalus means a moral behavior.
    ③ Tantalus concealed the secrets of the gods.
    ④ All the gods knew about Tantalus' misconduct.
    ⑤ Tantalus was a human who was closest to the gods.

| Words | Read the following definitions and find the words in the passage. |

• to grip or hold: _____
• to move back or backwards: _____
• an animal or person meant to be offered to a god: _____
• belonging or relating to the principles of good and evil, or right and wrong: _____
• to serve as a symbol or sign for something: _____

Read the following and answer the questions.

Have you ever worked for hours on a puzzle only to find that you're missing the final (a) <u>few pieces</u>? If you have, then you can understand the complex puzzle that is the evolution of humankind. Throughout history, scientists have tried to solve the mysterious puzzle of humankind's evolution.

Until the mid-1800's, most people firmly believed that humans had been created by God. However, Charles Robert Darwin, the naturalist who put forth the theory of evolution, brought this firmly-held belief into question.

In his 1871 publication, *The Descent of Man*, Darwin argued that humans had descended from ape-like creatures. Some people supported the idea but many other groups, including the Catholic Church, raised questions.

(b) <u>It was a hard pill to swallow after years of firm belief in creationism</u>. Also, they couldn't understand how man could evolve from apes because there were obvious missing links between the two. However, over time, many people accepted the idea and the search to find the "missing links" between humans and their ape-like ancestors began.

Initially, scientists believed that the evolution of man could be viewed as a progressing line of a species, each of which would look a little bit more like us. However, modern studies have shown that it is much more complex than that. It was earlier thought that humans originated in Asia, where giant ape-like fossils were found. However, in 1925, Dart discovered the fossil remains of an infant, human-like ape in the Transvaal region of South Africa. The similarity between the fossil and humans turned the spotlight to Africa. This discovery and others like it show that the origin of humanity must lie in Africa.

We have discovered a lot about the history of mankind since Darwin's time. Yet, there are still many mysteries to be solved. Thanks to the diligent and inventive minds of researchers, we are that much closer to finding the true "missing links."

1. What phrase has the same meaning as the underlined (a)
   in humankind's evolution? Find the phrase in the passage.

   _____

Impact reading

2. Which can be inferred from the underlined part (b)?

   ① Darwin's theory was too difficult to understand at that time.
   ② People believed Darwin's idea because he was a great doctor.
   ③ Darwin's theory was unbelievable due to a lack of scientific proof.
   ④ No one believed Darwin's theory because it was totally unreligious.
   ⑤ Darwin's theory was too radical for people who believed in God to accept.

3. Complete the summary by filling in the blanks with the given expressions.
   Change the form, if necessary.

evolution	fail	creation	achieve

   The mystery of mankind's _____ has been studied since
   Charles Robert Darwin questioned the belief that humans are the
   _____ of God. However, the idea _____ to
   explain some missing links between humans and apes, and researchers
   have been working hard to fill in these blanks with a great deal of
   _____ .

   Words   Read the following definitions and find the words in the passage.

   • a process of growth or advancement of a species: _____
   • a person who studies or an expert in natural history: _____
   • unchangeable, inflexible: _____
   • a primate species: _____
   • clearly evident: _____
   • to begin: _____
   • human parts that are found much later; for example, a bone or a skull: _____

A. Fill in the blanks with the appropriate words.

| crucial | extravagant | pandemic | recede | represents |

1. The _____ dinner party was for the millionaire's ten-year-old son.
2. Timing is _____ in dealing with relationship problems amongst employees.
3. The red rose in all of his paintings _____ his love for his wife.
4. Scientists warn that the mutant virus could cause a global _____ .
5. He sat on the shore watching the tide _____ .

B. Connect each expression in column A with the matching expression in column B.

A	B
1. make oneself at home •	• a. to maintain an equal rate of progress with others
2. keep up with •	• b. something unpleasant that must be tolerated
3. bring to life •	• c. to feel comfortable
4. a hard pill to swallow •	• d. direct attention to
5. turn the spotlight to •	• e. to put spirit into something

C. Fill in the blanks with the appropriate expressions.

1. She said that **the** _____ to her success was modesty.
   (= the most important reason for)
2. I'd never have the nerve **to just** _____ school like that. (= not go to)
3. That pile is for things that I plan to **throw** _____ . (= put in the garbage)
4. The new evidence **brings** his whole theory **into** _____ . (= creates doubt)

D. Complete each sentence with a hyphenated expression.

| ape- | firmly- | school- | held | like | phobic |

1. Some first graders are _____ at the beginning of the semester.

2. With the brown hood over his head, he looked rather _____.

3. It is my dad's _____ belief that boys are stronger than girls.

E. Choose the best word to complete each sentence.

1. A long time ago, _____ dogs became man's faithful companion.
   ① contributing   ② compiled   ③ problematic   ④ domesticated

2. She _____ having to tell her parents that she had failed math.
   ① dreaded   ② tantalized   ③ alerted   ④ originated

3. Years after his death, his _____ were shipped back home.
   ① struggles   ② remains   ③ sacrifices   ④ phobias

4. I have no _____ of ever speaking to him again.
   ① evolution   ② intention   ③ inspiration   ④ execution

5. The _____ of elderly parents should be severely dealt with.
   ① abandonment   ② misbehavior   ③ appetite   ④ psyche

Finding Corresponding Proverbs

Why are proverbs important?

- Traditional proverbs often represent a culture's values.
- Selecting a proverb related to the content of a certain text is used to test one's English reading comprehension ability.

• Usually this question is presented as follows.
  - Which saying best describes the writer's intention?
  - Which saying can be applied to the passage?

How to solve

1. Research common proverbs and memorize them.
2. Identify the main idea of the text by understanding its overall organization and flow.
3. Compare the given proverbs to the main idea of the text.

Common Proverbs

1. Look before you leap.
2. Practice makes perfect.
3. Many drops make a shower.
4. A stitch in time saves nine.
5. A good medicine tastes bitter.
6. All goes well that ends well.
7. Where there's a will, there's a way.
8. The pot calls the kettle black.
9. Don't count your chickens before they've hatched.
10. Do onto others as you would have them do onto you.

Actual Test

Read the passage and answer the following questions.

An Eskimo once told European visitors that the only true wisdom lives far from mankind, out in the great loneliness, and can be reached only through suffering. The great loneliness—like the loneliness a caterpillar endures when she wraps herself in a silky cocoon and begins the long transformation to butterfly. It seems that we too must go through such a time, when life as we have known it is over and yet we don't know who we are supposed to become. All we know is that something bigger is calling us to change. And though we must make the journey alone, and even if suffering is our only companion, soon enough we will become a butterfly, soon enough we will taste the joy of being alive.

step 1. Which word in the passage is used as a metaphor for human maturity that comes after going through a painful time?

_____

step 2. Choose the best proverb that expresses the main idea of the writing.

① Art is long. Life is short.
② A good medicine tastes bitter.
③ Failure teaches success.
④ Look before you leap.
⑤ Do onto others as you would have them do onto you.

Only the unreasonable man persists in trying to adapt the world to himself.
Therefore, all progress depends on the unreasonable man.
- George Bernard Shaw

Unit 5

Understanding Styles of Writing and Their Purpose

Read the following and answer the questions.

No one walks alone, and, when one is walking on the journey of life, just where do you start to thank those who joined you, walked beside you, and helped you along the way? Over the years, people that I have met and worked with have continually urged me (a)_____(write) a book, to put my thoughts down on paper, and to share my insights with others. So, at last, here it is.

Perhaps this book and its pages will be seen as a "thank you" to the thousands of people who have helped make my life what it is today.

First, I'd like to thank Jim, with whom I have had the pleasure of sharing a stage with. Over the years, his words have taught me much about myself and the mysterious ways of life.

I also need to thank Mark, a wonderful man who changed me completely. He taught me how to value the lives, thoughts, and expressions of others and how to understand and nurture their needs. Sadly he passed away, so my thanks go out to his family and all those around the world who loved him as much as I did.

And lastly, to my dear wife, Kelly, who has stood by me and kept me (b)_____(focus). Thank you my darling, you have been the inspiration that has driven me onwards.

I have poured my heart and soul into these pages, so now I pray that my words touch your heart, soul, and mind.

Words   Read the following definitions and translate them into Korean.

- **urge:** to persuade or encourage someone to do something _____
- **insight:** the ability to gain a deep understanding of the real, often hidden situation _____
- **nurture:** to care for _____
- **inspiration:** something that stimulates the mind, especially to artistic activity. _____
- **onward:** moving forward in place or time _____

Impact reading

1. What style of writing is this?

① Book review
② Travel journal
③ Acknowledgement
④ Newsletter
⑤ Cover letter

2. What are the most appropriate word forms for blanks (a) and (b)? Use the given words.

(a) _____   (b) _____

3. Write T if the statement is true. Write F if it is false.

① The writer expresses his thanks to many people including one who is already dead. _____

② The author's peers encouraged him to write the book. _____

③ The writer's wife continually distracted him from his writing. _____

TIP

Prolific Writers

+ How long do you think it takes to write a book? For most writers, it takes months or even years to write a book. However, some writers have written hundreds of books in their lives. Mary Faulkner, ranked as the most prolific novelist in the Guinness Book of World Records, wrote 904 books. On the other hand, there are writers who only wrote a single book in their whole life. Harper Lee wrote the Pulitzer winning novel *To Kill a Mockingbird* and it was her only major work.

Read the following and answer the questions.

Welcome to Happy Kids Therapy Center

Are your children:

Getting angry too often or being disrespectful or defiant?

Struggling with school problems? Experiencing anxiety, clingy behavior, or shyness?

Having difficulty coping with divorce or other family problems?

Lacking self-confidence or experiencing low self-esteem?

Suffering from something traumatic that happened to them?

We can help you understand your children!! We can help them grow!!
HKTC is a child-centered, family focused treatment center. Childhood should be the best time of one's life and children deserve the chance to reach their full potential. As the old saying "_____" suggests, children who have happy childhoods are more likely to become positive contributors to a healthy society.

Our Mission: To help children reach their full potential and celebrate their unique strengths, our therapists provide comprehensive treatment using a variety of techniques such as play therapy and speech therapy. Through playing with their peers, group building activities, and various educational toys, children are encouraged to develop their ability to express emotions and interpersonal communication skills. Speech therapy will also improve each child's success with communication, peer activities, and self help skills. Our therapists have extensive training and experience treating children. For an appointment or a free telephone consultation, call (913) 638-6200 today!

| Words | Read the following definitions and translate them into Korean. |

- **disrespectful**: being rude to another person _____
- **defiant**: refusing to do something asked of one _____
- **self-esteem**: a person's value or opinion of themselves _____
- **comprehensive**: covering all aspects of something _____
- **interpersonal**: involving relationships between different people _____
- **therapist**: a person who helps deal with a personal problem or condition _____

Impact reading

1. What style of writing is this passage?

① Ad for a therapy center
② Official document of HKTC
③ Newsletter for nursery teachers
④ News article for child education
⑤ Application form for a therapy center

2. Which is NOT mentioned in this passage?

① The office hours of HKTC
② Who needs to enroll in HKTC
③ What services the center provides
④ What qualifications the therapists have
⑤ The benefits that children will enjoy through various therapies

3. What is the most appropriate saying for the blank?

① Every dog has its day.
② Monkey see, monkey do.
③ One swallow can't make a summer.
④ Treat others as you would wish to be treated by them.
⑤ You can lead a horse to water but you can't make it drink.

TIP

ADHD

+ Quite a lot of parents are worried that their children might have ADHD. Attention Deficit Hyperactivity Disorder, ADHD is without question one of the most common conditions that affects a large number of children. Children who have ADHD find it very hard to pay attention. They are easily distracted and it makes it hard for them to concentrate.

Read the following and answer the questions.

May. 13, 2005

(a) _____

Seoul, May 13, 2005, Sonit Electronics, a leader in consumer electronics, announced its unedited consolidated earnings results for the three month period ending March 31, 2005.

On a global basis, both sales and operating profits soared to record-high levels, thanks to stable operations from all business divisions, mainly resulting from (b) robust sales in handsets and flat panel TVs. Sales jumped 16.9% in one year to USD 11.747 billion, with an operating profit of USD 634 million. This makes the profit margin 5.4%, higher than the 5.1% recorded the previous year.

On a parent basis, first-quarter sales rose 14.8% from the previous year. Net Profile boasted strong profits of USD 442 million, successfully recovering from a loss of $131 million a year earlier.

The Mobile Communications Company achieved record-high sales, up 32.6% from the first quarter, 2004. Handset sales are up 35.7% since last year. Shipments of handsets recorded the highest in unit sales as well, a total of 24.4 million, thanks to strong cell phone sales.

Shipments to emerging markets including Asia, China and the Middle East increased 36% this quarter, while sales in the US and Korea increased 18%.

Sales from the Digital Media Company dropped 5.2% last year, but operating profit margins have increased to $18 million, up 1.3% due to cost innovations in the PC industry.

Words

Read the following definitions and translate them into Korean.

- **unedited:** not edited or revised _____
- **consolidated:** brought together into a single whole _____
- **margin:** the difference between the cost and the selling price _____
- **quarter:** one of the four equal three month periods into which the fiscal year can be divided _____

Impact reading

1. What style of writing is this passage?

① Newsletter
② Cover letter
③ Quarterly report
④ Fashion magazine article
⑤ Electronic devices price list

2. What is the most appropriate expression for the blank (a)?

① Sonit Electronic's Annual Report
② Sonit Electronics Reports A New Market for 2005
③ Sonit Electronics Reports New Models for Next Year
④ Sonit Electronics Reports Slow Growth of Earnings
⑤ Sonit Electronics Reports First Quarter 2005 Earnings Results

3. What can replace the underlined part (b)? Find the word in the passage.

_____

TIP

Stockholder

+ How can you make a profit by buying and selling stocks? Basically, stocks represent a share of ownership in a corporation. By buying that, you became stockholder, one of the owners of the company. If the company makes a profit, the price of its stock goes up. Therefore, buy stocks when the price is low and sell when the price is high.

Dear Michael the Money Man,

I've been reading your column on financial advice for two years and I'm dying to know your opinion on art as an investment. My husband keeps buying Chinese pottery and contemporary paintings expecting that they will be a good investment. He is spending too much of our savings on artwork. Last year, his co-worker bought some artwork and made a lot of money off of it. But I'm still cynical. Is investing in art really safe?

From,
Nervous in New York

Dear Nervous in New York,

Thanks for your letter. This topic is nothing new in the investment world. Fine art has become one of the most common investments over the last hundred years. However, selling art is not always as easy as trading on the London or New York Stock Exchange.

Rather than buying individual pieces, it is better to invest in a fund. The UK-based Fine Art Fund is a more stable and safe way to invest in artwork. The fund invests in anything from old masters to contemporary pieces. The idea is the same as when investors pool their money together to buy stocks or bonds. Only this time, they are buying art. This allows you more flexibility and (a)_____.

If you choose this avenue you could be looking at as much as a 10~15% return on your investment over a three year period. While I wouldn't advise you to run out straight away to the nearest gallery, there is some truth to what your husband is saying, and art has served as a worthwhile and stable investment for thousands of people.

Yours Truly,
Michael the Money Man

Impact reading

1. For what purpose did "Nervous in New York" write this letter?

① To get information on stable art funds
② To get information on qualified fund investors
③ To ask for advice on how to identify authentic Chinese pottery
④ To make sure her family's investment strategy is a good one
⑤ To ask for better ways to persuade her husband not to invest money in art

2. What is the most appropriate expression for the blank (a)?

① you can get various kinds of artwork
② you can minimize investment risk
③ you don't have to rely on online investments only
④ your return on your savings will be greater than before
⑤ your money will also be invested in buying stocks and bonds

3. Which best describes the advisor's attitude towards investing in an art fund.

① cynical
② supportive
③ critical
④ ambiguous
⑤ indecisive

| Words | Read the following definitions and find the words in the passage. |

• putting money into a stock or fund in order to make a profit: _____
• of the present time; modern: _____
• money invested or contributed for some special purpose: _____
• to put resources or money into a group investment: _____
• an ability to change and adapt to new circumstances: _____
• a method or way to accomplish something: _____

Read the following and answer the questions.

A trip to Machu Picchu can be a thrilling experience for historians and travel buffs alike. It was constructed around 1450, at the height of the Inca Empire. Most visitors are surprised that it was built on the most wild and inaccessible mountain area available. It remains a mystery how the Incas were able to carry huge blocks of stone to the top of the mountain and build such a spectacular culture. It is assumed that this place was constructed as the traditional birthplace of the Inca people, or possibly as a prison for those who had committed heinous crimes.

Machu Picchu was designated a World Heritage Site in 1983 and selected as one of the New Seven Wonders of the World in 2007 for its architectural mastery and unique testimony to the Inca civilization. However, this world heritage site has been threatened by the impact of tourism and uncontrolled development around it. For example, the construction of a cable car to the ruins as well as the development of a luxury hotel and a tourist complex with boutiques and restaurants has damaged the nature around the site and influenced the natives' lives. In addition, natural threats such as fires and landslides have posed additional serious hazards to the site.

Many scientists, scholars, and the Peruvian public are extremely concerned about the influence of economic and commercial forces on this special place. Some damage to the site due to heavy usage has already occurred. For this reason, UNESCO is considering putting Machu Picchu on its list of endangered World Heritage Sites. However, this move could backfire by drawing even more visitors to this site, creating a massive physical burden on the ruins. If people don't pay enough attention to preserving Machu Picchu, one of the world's most enchanting historical sites will disappear forever.

Impact reading

1. What is the main purpose of the passage?

① To report the development of Machu Picchu
② To appreciate one of the World Heritage sites
③ To complain about the facilities at Machu Picchu
④ To introduce the New Seven Wonders of the World
⑤ To warn people about damage to a famous historical site

2. Which is NOT true about Machu Picchu?

① It might have been used to isolate criminals from society.
② It is a good place to enjoy both historical ruins and nature.
③ It was designated a World Heritage Site but may soon be endangered.
④ It is guessed that people in Machu Picchu died from a contagious disease.
⑤ Tourism and economic development have had bad influences on Machu Picchu.

3. Complete the summary by filling in the blanks with the given expressions. Change the form, if necessary.

enchant	incur	destroy	influx	appear

Machu Piccu is a wonderful site to see, but an _____ of visitors and development around the site have had _____ results on this _____ place. If this continues, Machu Picchu will _____ even more damage and may even _____ forever.

Words   Read the following definitions and find the words in the passage.

• to accept something without proof; to take for granted: _____
• extremely wicked or evil: _____
• to name, choose or specify someone or something for a particular purpose or duty: _____
• to make or be a threat to someone or something: _____
• a strong effect or impression: _____
• to have the opposite result to the one intended: _____

A. Fill in the blanks with the appropriate words.

| defiant | flexibility | urge | value | threaten |

1. This exercise program is guaranteed to help increase your _____ .
2. Your grandfather would _____ you to learn more about various cultures.
3. Jack stood in front of the teacher with a _____ look on his face.
4. A furious dog next door _____ s me all the time.
5. This whole ordeal has made me _____ our friendship even more.

B. Match the underlined phrases with their meanings.

| a. died | b. is caused by | c. fighting | d. supported |

1. His fear of dogs results from a bad childhood experience. _____
2. I was sorry to hear that the old man had passed away. _____
3. She is the one person that stood by me through it all. _____
4. She has been struggling with weight problems since forever. _____

C. Fill in the blanks with the appropriate expressions.

1. Our store **was designated** _____ an emergency shelter. (= chosen to be)
2. The simple design was basically **lacking** _____ creativity. (= did not have)
3. I **am dying** _____ find out what happens in the next episode.(= want very much to)
4. The band split up **at the height** _____ their popularity. (= at the highest level of)
5. I hear she is slowly **recovering** _____ her operation. (= becoming well after)

D. Fill in the blanks with the appropriate words in the box. Change the form, if necessary.

| access | appear | control | unedit | respectful |

1. The studio announced that an _____ copy of the film has been found.

2. The remote temple high up in the mountains is _____ by car.

3. The children watched in awe as the magician made the rabbit _____ .

4. His speech was about how the _____ spread of guns affects society.

5. It is _____ to others to talk loudly on your cell phone in public places.

E. Choose the best word to complete each sentence.

1. She often chooses books that provide _____ into human relationships.
   ① insights   ② expressions   ③ inspiration   ④ self-esteem

2. This is a _____ list of all the supplies that will be needed for the event.
   ① clingy   ② interpersonal   ③ comprehensive   ④ consolidated

3. He was voted the new chairman by a _____ of 54 votes to 46.
   ① division   ② margin   ③ basis   ④ fund

4. He became rich by making some good stock _____.
   ① avenues   ② developments   ③ impacts   ④ investments

5. The neighbors decided to _____ their money to rebuild the center.
   ① pour   ② reach   ③ serve   ④ pool

Understanding Styles of Writing and Their Purpose

Introduction

These types of questions test the readers' ability to grasp the purpose of the writing.
Thus, it is important to be able to approach the writing with a holistic view.

How to solve

1. Identify the main idea of the writing.

2. Look for the sentence that contains the writer's intention.

3. It is important to identity the type and the purpose of the writing.

4. Look for repetitive words or phrases.

Plus tips

• Keep the following types of writing in mind, for they are the ones usually used in these types of questions.

1. **Informative:** there are explanations of new information

2. **Travel journal:** the journey of one's trip is described throughout the writing.

3. **Advertisements:** unfamiliar proper nouns such as brands or product names appear in the writing.

4. **Articles:** the writing is presented from an objective point of view.
   - In general, this style of writing uses formal expressions before getting to the point.

Actual Test

Read the passage and answer the following questions.

It is my great pleasure to inform you that your sons and daughters have completed all the academic requirements over the last three years of study at Hutt High School. We feel as if the day they entered our school were yesterday, and now they will proudly receive their graduation certificates. Not unlike many successful graduates in our long history, your children will go out into the world, and successfully participate in the fields of politics, economics, culture, and education. The graduation ceremony will be held next Friday in Hutt High School's Assembly Hall. On behalf of the school, I would like to extend our invitation to you and your family. I look forward to meeting you there.

step 1. Find the main topic of this passage.

_____

step 2. Fill in each blank according to the relationship between 'I' and 'you' in the text.

I : _____   you : _____

step 3. Choose the purpose of the passage.

① To ask someone to give a congratulatory speech
② To inform the schedule of the entrance ceremony
③ To invite someone to their own child's graduation ceremony
④ To inform the qualifications for getting admission to school
⑤ To hold a school committee meeting

MEMO

MEMO